Laura Turok-Ellis

Shockey
Copyright © 2025 by Laura Turok–Ellis

ISBN: 979-8895311660 (sc)
ISBN: 979-8895311677 (e)

All rights reserved. No part of this publication may be reproduced, distributed, or transmitted in any form or by any means, including photocopying, recording, or other electronic or mechanical methods, without the prior written permission of the publisher and/or the author, except in the case of brief quotations embodied in critical reviews and other noncommercial uses permitted by copyright law.

The views expressed in this book are solely those of the author and do not necessarily reflect the views of the publisher, and the publisher hereby disclaims any responsibility for them.

Writers' Branding
(877) 608-6550
www.writersbranding.com
media@writersbranding.com

Dedication

To Pam, who first read my book; Sue, who encouraged me with Friday morning cappuccinos and late night black and white movies; Lynda S., who helped me find my voice on the page; Cindy, who is the world's best cheerleader (not to mention devil's advocate); Gail, who always believed I could be a successful writer, and my children, Christina, Riley and Charles.

Contents

Chapter One 1
Chapter Two 5
Chapter Three 11
Chapter Four 15
Chapter Five 21
Chapter Six 26
Chapter Seven 29
Chapter Eight 33
Chapter Nine 38
Chapter Ten 44
Chapter Eleven 48
Chapter Twelve 53
Author Biography 57

Chapter One

I HATE MOVING, even though in my relatively short life, I've had to move eleven times already! I really hate changing schools, though, and this year for Christmas, I got a real double whammy when my dad announced that we were moving during the holiday break.

Let me back up a little first and explain about my family. My father is an artist. He does sculpting work, but he does it on commission. He's good enough to have plenty of work, but instead of having a studio, he travels wherever his works of art are desired. Wherever the wind blows, it seems.

When we were younger it was an exciting venture moving from town to town. But, when my sisters were old enough to start school, Eleanor, my oldest sister, began protesting. Soon my middle sister, Agnes, developed ain't-movin'-itis, too. They complain a lot, but we still keep moving.

My mom, Rita, is called Rita because she doesn't like the moniker 'Mom' and believes that she'll be discovered like some big hotshot actress from the Stone Age, Rita Hayworth. Anyway, Rita-mom drifts in and out of our lives, depending on how successful she has been.

This Christmas, she actually showed up with presents, even if they were a little odd and even if she was one short. It was beginning to shape up to be a real holiday when my dad hatched his plan.

The day we got out of school, my dad called a 'family meeting.' Pretty unusual if you consider we four kids have raised ourselves. Oh, he paid the rent and bought groceries, but we learned early on that we were our own best help. We stuck together and made sure the rent payments were relatively on time and that the groceries he brought home (or sent us after) were relatively healthy.

"I need to talk to all of you!" I remember my dad yelling as he rushed through the front door, slamming it loudly behind him.

"You mean a 'family meeting'?" Eleanor responded with not just a little irritation in her voice. "Families have 'family' meetings!" she added with a huff, then returned to her kitchen duties.

"A girl at my school says they have family meetings every night at their house." Abbey, the youngest sister, chimed in. "Right after dinner!"

"Oh, and I suppose that's why we don't have them because we rarely have a family dinner!" Agnes was just adding fuel to the fire.

I couldn't stand it, "Oh, shut up! All of you!" Abbey began to tear up, Eleanor threw her kitchen towel to the couch and Agnes just rolled her eyes.

We didn't have the best dad in town but he was at least there for us. That was more than I could usually say for mom, ahem, Rita.

"Let's just let dad speak," I mumbled.

"Thanks, Shockey." That's what my dad called me 'Shockey', "I have some great news and we're all going to love it. Even you, Miriam,' that was my mother's real name and my dad said he refused to call her anything else no matter how famous she got. "Seems as if that last sculpture I did for the city of Paducah was very well received and we're moving to Kentucky!"

You could have heard a pin drop on cotton the room got so quite. Eleanor buried her head in her hands and ran to the kitchen, Agnes just continued rolling her eyes. Abbey tried to cuddle up to Rita-mom why the family hasn't been to Pad u carlton had already done a scupture there being only slightly rebuffed and asked "Where's Ken-ucky?" She was five and had just started kindergarten. Her concept of the world was our backyard and the five-block walk to school.

"Ken Tücky," began my dad, "is a wonderful state about a day's drive from here, and it's full of bluegrass and horses!"

"Blue grass?" Agnes' interest had been piqued. "Whoever heard of bluegrass?!"

Shockey

"I have and it's real." Now Eleanor had come from the kitchen to rejoin the group. "It's not really blue, it's just the color it looks when the sun shines on it a certain way."

"Hey! You're a smart girl! Just like your old man!" My dad was giving himself way too much credit. "We're leaving the day after Christmas so we can get settled before a new school semester starts!"

My dad initiated our famous family group hug and that was that.

My sisters and I had spent our whole lives travelling up and down the Eastern seaboard between Flagler Beach, Florida and Cape Fear, North Carolina and any little artsy coves and cays between. My father had dragged us to arts and crafts fields since we were old enough to walk. Most of my life had been spent in South Carolina between Myrtle Beach and Beaufort with a lot of time DI Charleston in between. Charleston is a hotbed of artsy activity and my dad spent untold hours smolzzhg with that crowd. Heck, I'd even been to a couple of Spoleto events, but watching grown men Prance around in tights or listening to recitations in the park aren't exactly what I call a good day's fun.

I don't remember my mom ever really being a part of the group. Oh, she'd pop up once in a while about every six months or so. That's kind of how Abbey became one of us. My mom and dad were married in one of those new-age ceremonies where the couples promise to stand side-by-side and share the world but when mom became pregnant with Eleanor she apparently decided that motherhood was not for her. At least the parts of motherhood that come after childbirth. Agnes came about 18 months later and then a quick two years later I was born. My father called me 'Shockey' because he was shocked that I had been a boy. My given name is Elliot but for as long as I can remember my dad has called me 'Shockey'. I'm kinda used to it now. Abbey was another story altogether. Rita-mom had been absent for nearly a year when she returned for the longest period that I ever remember her staying with us. Abigail showed up that year. It didn't occur to me until several years later, and after a few health classes, that Abbey was the shortest pregnancy on record. My dad never said anything and has always treated her the same as the rest of us.

I guess he didn't put two and two together or just didn't care. It's that new-age kind of existence.

Christmas was surreal. We'd never really gone to church so we were missing the gist of Christmas to begin with. Rita-mom with her gifts blew in and then left as quickly as she'd come. I didn't really think she was going with us but I had hoped. The day of the move was just like so many of the others. We got up, picked through what we wanted to take with us, filled the trunk of the car with clothing and a few pots and pans, said good-bye to the apartment and left. In all the moves I'd made I never remembered taking any furniture with us. Not one picture. Not one potted plant. Of course, in our household a plant wouldn't have a chance of survival anyway.

Chapter Two

THE DRIVE TO was, to say the least, educational.

We passed through the Great Smokey Mountains, North Carolina, Tennessee and finally Kentucky. It wasn't the bluegrass part of the state like Dad had said. He'd painted a pretty picture to get us excited about this move. Florida, South Carolina, Georgia, and North Carolina; those were all southern states. They had beaches, hot weather, and seafood that I could relate to. Kentucky? We rolled into a little berg named Eddyville and found a roadside diner. Right away, we noticed that things were going to be different. The people talked funny. It was a lazy speech with no 'Rs' and a diphthong at the end of every syllable. Hill became Hee-uhl and light turned into li-at, as in "I'm gonna turn o-wuff the frunt po-wuch li-at." It was kinda funny, especially since I wasn't going to be living in Eddyville (pronounced Eddy-vee-uhl).

The waitress was nice enough. She offered up water glasses and menus and began cooing over Abbey.

"This is the sweetest little angel-babuhee I evuh laid eyes on. Whatcha name, sugah?" The waitress grinned at Abbey and tweaked her cheek like a long-lost aunt.

"Abigail, ma'am," Abbey softly replied, "But everybody calls me Abbey."

The waitress turned to walk away, but Abbey had post to make, "4nd ma'am?" Abbey was Pounhg on the southern accent, she was going to fit nkhtz)? here. "Ma'am, lazz't no bay-bee!" The emphasis was only s/zkht/y on 'bay.'

The waitress just grinned and said she'd be back to take our orders. We all took our own sweet time looking over the selections on the gravy-spattered placards. It was the usual fare, fried chicken, mashed potatoes, BLTs, eggs, bacon and hash browns. What no grits? We were truly in a foreign country! I don't think a single week of my whole life had gone by without having grits. But grits were the least of our worries. We ordered and Selma, our waitress who we were getting to know about like our own Rita-mom, promised to bring us the best peCAHN pie we'd ever tasted. Right away Agnes wanted to know if peCAHNs were as tasty as PEE-cans. Selma just giggled and skillfully brought us our orders. She even brought extra ice cream for Abbey. That made her grin and exclaim that she liked Ken-ucky better than any town she'd ever lived in.

The town we were headed to was called Paducah. It was on the Ohio River and apparently had a long and storied past concerning the Civil War (an event known only as the War of Northern Aggression farther south). I wasn't sure what to expect, but I was an experienced NKOB (new kid on the block) so I knew what to say and do and what not to say and what not to do. Of course, no matter how many times you move and how much you know about being new, you're still new. And it hurts.

On the drive into Paducah I had time to think about things and how I wanted to reinvent myself this time. It was a little game I played. No harm meant. It's just that when you move as often as I have you never really make any real friends and any lies you accidentally tell to get yourself out of hot water, rarely have time to catch up with you. As it was, my dad was having to telephone our old school to have our records sent to Kentucky. I doubt we would even be able to start back on the first day of the semester. But, that wasn't all bad either.

It took about 45 minutes from Eddyville to Paducah and in through the front door of our motel room. It was called the Hinkleville Road Motel and seemed to be fashioned after one of those Route 66, B-movie thriller-type motels, you know them: one story, faded paint job, flashing half-lit neon sign. At first glance I half expected a man with a chazz saw 10 come from behind the office door, but once I gave it a second glance, it wasn't a bad place after all. And actually, all the neon in the sign worked. It didn't hide the fact that I was thrilled to be living in a place that had a business attached to the name 'Hinkleville'. I didn't even want to ask about the name, but I was sure I would find out sooner or later. The motel was clean enough and had cable TV, something we never had in our apartments. There were two full-size beds, one for Eleanor and Agnes, one for me and Dad and poor Abbey was going to have to sleep on the floor, again. I looked around the room. It was pretty fair-sized for a motel. And by now I was quite the expert on temporary sleeping arrangements. Usually, we got thrown into some mangy hole-in-the-wall for a week or two until Dad could find something more permanent. You know the type, the ones with the floral bedspreads straight from the 1960s with paintings on the wall to match. The rooms almost always smelled of old cigars and feet. Personally, I kept my shoes on except for when I was in the shower. I just didn't trust the germs that went with the smells in most motels. This one was different. It didn't smell like cigars and better yet, it didn't smell of feet. I was pleasantly surprised that there were bedspreads with horses and paintings that didn't match! The drapes were even a bit tasteful. At least, that's what Eleanor said. She'd gone around the room with a can of disinfectant spraying every surface she could to ward off the germs of strangers. Before any of us could really get settled, a knock came at the door.

"Don't open it!" dad warned. "I'll get it! You just never know who you're going to run into." He walked to the door, peered out the peep hole, then turned and smiled as he opened the door. "It's just the motel owner, Mr. Parks!" He grinned at us like he was introducing his bestfriend, then turned to the man and said "Come in! Come in! I want you to meet my family!"

There was that word again. Family.

"Why hello, folks!" Mr. Parks was a little rotund, but very jovial. He sort of chuckled when he spoke and he was always smiling. It was a good kind of smile, though. Some motel managers where we've stayed seemed to be angry all the time, as if it were a prerequisite for the job. Mr. Parks seemed genuinely happy and even a little kind. Of course, he came in carrying a big basket that smelled like heaven, so I guess I should say he seemed a lot kind!

"Ginny thought you'd be hungry coming in at the dinner hour, so she sent over some meatloaf, mashed 'taters, and cornbread. She's got some dessert baking right now, but you folks'll have to wait about an hour for that. It'll give this food time to settle!" Mr. Parks came in, set down the basket and turned to dad, "Now I got a jug of ice tea in the office, but Ginny wants me to ask if you want sugar in it?"

Sugar? In tea? Well, duh! Who would ever think of drinking ice tea without sugar?

"You know up here, we don't use a lot of sugar in our drinks unless it's lemonade or a mint julep, but then you folks is a might young to know about mint juleps!" Mr. Parks tapped dad on the shoulder, "Well, maybe not you, Mr. Wallace." Then he headed for the door chuckling louder, apparently amused at his own little joke. "I'll have Kenny run the tea over, do you have enough cups? Oh, the ice machine is not quite working right, but I've got a load of ice on the way and I'll have Kenny bring you a bag as soon as it gets here."

"Sweet, please, Mr. Parks" Eleanor piped up to announce that we drank our tea with sugar. "And, if you have a straw for the baby, that would be nice!"

"Why certainly," Mr. Parks responded. "But, honey, that 'baby' looks old enough to be in school now!" And more chuckling parted Mr. Parks' lips as he gently pulled the door to behind him on his exit.

"I ain't no baby! I'm five and I am going to school! How many babies you know that go to school, huh, Ellie?" Abby was adamant that she would be included in the school plans that dad had to make, but more so I think she was just reminding us that she was here.

Another tap at the door and Agnes jumped up to the curtains, peeking outside then swinging the door open to reveal a boy about my age or older, holding a pitcher of tea. "Hey, daddy said to bring this to you." He almost grunted, his voice was so low, but maybe it was the way he was hanging his head, "And, these, too" he thrust some straws at Agnes, then turned to walk away, stopped and looked back over his shoulder. "The roll-away bed won't be ready for another hour. Daddy wants to know if that'll be alright?" He shoved his hands in his pocket, stared off to the right, then glanced back, waiting for an answer.

"Sure, a roll-away would be great, whenever it gets here." Agnes was talking softer than I'd ever heard and the tell-tale sweep of the hair over her shoulder made me think she was being a little flirtatious, too. "Of course, we're going to need some assistance putting it together." She smiled. Well, I couldn't see her, but I knew she was smiling, just by the way she was playing with the edge of the welcome mat with her sock covered toe. "I can send Shockey to help, if you need." She was sure quick to offer me up for work, why didn't she go get the darned thing herself, then maybe she and motel-boy could stroll for a romantic walk by the interstate. Heck, one of 'em might even get hit! That would sure liven up the scene a bit!

"Oh, and tell your momma that we sure appreciate the food. We are all just star-ving!" She emphasized the 'star' as if we hadn't eaten for days. And everyone of us had eaten a full meal at the "Park and Dine" in Eddyville less than two hours earlier!

"Oh, no problem," motel-boy replied. "She likes to cook and does that for all our guests because we ain't got no diner close by."

Actually, there was a Mickey D'S just up the road and something called Burger Chef down the other way. I doubt we would've starved regardless. But the home cooking was going to taste good in about an hour, when my stomach was empty again and I was knocked back watching a good movie on HBO. Besides, at least I knew someone in Paducah now, even if he was the motel owner's son. Maybe he would go to the same school. That would be a first for me, actually knowing someone before I stepped foot into a social situation.

As I closed the door I noticed the wind was picking up a little and it was beginning to feel like winter again. We had all wondered what the weather would be like. We passed snow in the mountains and icy rain in Tennessee, but since we'd been in Kentucky, we'd barely worn jackets. I watched through the gap in the drapes as motel-boy fell back toward the office and thought about yelling after him. I was hungry for some male companionship. Being around girls all the time can get on a fella's last nerve. My dad was hardly company. He was taking inventory of his sculpting supplies, and Eleanor helped him make a list of what he needed. Abbey was snooping in the basket of goodies and squealed when she discovered brownies and Agnes was all dreamy-eyed over motel-boy. It was going to be a long night except that if there were already brownies in the basket, what did Mrs. Parks consider dessert? I licked my lips in anticipation, then hopped on the bed dad and I would share, grabbed the remote and started flipping channels.

"Hey, look, we've got the Disney Channel!" Abbey squealed again, came over and plopped down beside me with a big brownie in her mits and we cuddled up to watch "The Shaggy Detective." Me and the baby who wasn't a baby anymore. Wow, just like home.

Chapter Three

A COUPLE OF days had passed when dad came 'home' one afternoon and announced that we were all going to a New Year's Eve party with the Parks family. Great. Just the way I've always wanted to celebrate; my dad, my three sisters, a motel owner and his family and me. I couldn't imagine the fun I'd be having. Wow, just like home. But, the bright side was that at least I would be getting out to do something. The trip had pretty much drained our finances and dad wasn't expecting a payment for his work until after the first of the year. We were okay. Mr. Parks had made an agreement that we could pay for our stay at the motel by helping with some of the chores. Eleanor and Agnes were helping Mrs. Parks clean rooms and even Abbey was helping to organize brochures in the office. For a dinky little roadside motel, the Parks' did okay by it. There was a constant flow of traffic in and out. Being next to the interstate had it's advantages. Me, I got to help motel-boy do the physical stuff, like moving roll-away beds in and out of rooms; stocking ice because the ice machine was still acting weird and sweeping the sidewalks and parking lot to keep up appearances. The Parks' were in direct competition with some major hotel chains, but because their rates were so reasonable, and apparently Mrs. Parks' cooking was earning a reputation with businessmen, there was never a lack of clientele. Motel-boy was quiet like me. We didn't talk much but occasionally he would tell a joke about a customer or his parents and we'd laugh for a minute or two between jobs. Once we watched a woman stroll across the parking lot and motel-boy mumbled, "There goes Wilma." I didn't quite understand, but he was chuckling so I had to get in on the joke.

"Who's Wilma?" 1 asked.

"Oh, you know, Wilma Flintstone," he answered, "Her husband looks just like Barney so I call her Wilma."

"But, Wilma's husband was Fred," I replied with a puzzled expression. How could anybody mix up Wilma and Betty? Betty was the cute one, and Wilma was the smart one.

"Yeah, I know that," motel-boy said, "But, I don't think that Barney is really her husband!" he grinned at me then continued, "You get to see all kinds of stuff living around a motel."

I figured it had to be some great entertainment watching people come and go.

"Wilma and Barney come in about every 60 days," motel-boy explained, "But they always arrive in separate cars." Motel-boy was pretty observant.

"I guess that's a dead giveaway," I added. But where is Barney right now?"

"Oh, he's some kind of traveling salesman and he has accounts here in Paducah and across the river in Metropolis." Motel-boy was losing interest in the topic, but he continued, "He's been coming here for about three years now, but Wilma just started joining him last year sometime."

My interest was increasing but motel-boy quickly changed the subject when a delivery truck showed up. Triangle Ice was painted all over the side and I knew we'd be hoisting five-pound bags of ice the rest of the afternoon. Every room was filled with either businessmen coming or going home, or partiers with New Year's reservations at the Bluegrass Convention Center located just down the street. All the hotels and motels on this strip were offering special room rates and limousine service for New Year's Eve to and from the convention center. Turns out that that was where we were going, too. Things were looking up for Shockey Wallace for the first time in a long time.

Motel-boy and I moved bags of ice for about three hours that afternoon and as the sun set, the air temperature began going down, too. During the day we enjoyed 50 degree weather, much like in South Carolina, but at night the temperatures dipped to below 30 degrees and it was dipping fast tonight. I was wearing my jacket because grabbing bags of ice, even in 50 degree weather, can chill you to the bone. The last bag was secured inside the chest freezer the Parks' kept for emergencies like this and after shutting the lid, motel-boy hopped up on top, pulled a pack of cigarettes from his pocket and fired one up.

"Want one?" he shoved the pack my direction.

"Nah, never tried it but I don't think I want to." I said

"Come on, what's it gonna hurt?" motel-boy didn't seem to be the kind of guy who would take no for an answer.

"Well, okay," and I reached for the pack but motel-boy jerked it back quickly.

"Hey, I'm not gonna start you on a bad habit, just bein' polite, that's all." He grinned with the cigarette tucked neatly on the side of his mouth.

"No, that's okay, I'll try one. Besides," I countered, "What's it gonna hurt?"

Motel-boy smiled, pushed the pack back at me and gently shook one cancer-stick at me. I took it and leaned forward for a light.

"Hey, don't inhale too much the first drag or it'll make you cough your fool head OR.' Motel-boy was being honest, but I inhaled so deeply that I think I coughed up one of my toenails.

"See, I told ya!" He removed the cigarette from his lips with his thumb and forefinger like they do in the movies then let a stream of smoke escape through his pursed lips. "Now watch this," he put the cigarette back between his lips only this time at the front of his mouth and I watched as he inhaled so deeply I thought the insides of his cheeks would touch. Then he made an exaggerated 'O' with his mouth and made a soft huffing sound. I watched in amazement as little 'O's of smoke left his mouth. Smoke rings! He'd made smoke rings! I wanted to smoke if only to do that, so I took another drag off my own cigarette and mimicked what motel-boy had done. Instead of cool little smoke rings, I regurgitated the contents of my late afternoon snack all over the floor of his parents' storage room. Fortunately I hadn't eaten more than a pack of peanut butter crackers so there wasn't much of a mess to clean up. Fortunately, I had also amused the hell out of motel-boy, and he even offered to help me clean up. I put out the cigarette on the floor next to my former snack then proceeded to sprinkle the whole mess with a can full of sta-dri from the bag that was kept in the corner.

"Yga, we've always got some guest hurling something," took it all in stride. "My dad buys that stuff by the 50 pound sack. Good thing, huh?"

"Oh, this was a good thing all right." I was embarrassed, but hotel-boy just slapped me on the back and offered some advice.

"Let's just keep the smoking between us. I don't want my dad thinking I'm corrupting you and frankly, I don't want to share my cigarettes with a candy ass!" He laughed, I blushed, then chuckled and before you know it we were both chortling as if we'd heard the funniest joke ever.

"By the way," I ventured, "Where'd you get those cigarettes anyway? You're not old enough to buy them and I know your mom and dad don't smoke."

Motel-boy just looked at me as if I was an alien. "Man, some guest left 'em. You wouldn't believe the stuff I get to keep because some careless customer drives off without it!"

And that's how I got in more trouble than I've ever been in my life. I couldn't even blame motel-boy. Of course, it wouldn't have done any good if I had.

Chapter Four

NEW YEAR'S EVE was going to be fun this year. The morning started out okay. Mr. Parks let us all have the day off, he and his wife had hired a relative to watch the desk for them so that we could all make the party. Motel-boy and I did clean up a couple of rooms in case they were needed at the last minute, but mostly, we lounged around the poolside. It was a warm 65 degrees and the weatherman had claimed that this was turning out to be one of the warmest winters in more than 20 years. Eleanor was reading a copy of the Louisville Courier-Journal she'd gotten from a guest who was on his way to Nashville. Agnes was mooning over the fact that I spent all my time with motel-boy and that left her no time to flirt. I didn't have the heart to tell her that motel-boy wasn't exactly interested in hewI figured she'd find that out soon enough. Abbey was content to play with the doll that Rita-mom had given her for Christmas and Dad and the Parks' were plotting a move for us from the hotel to a residential section of town that Mrs. Parks had been scouting. Frankly, I was content staying where we were, but Dad wanted to get us settled before school started. Mrs. Parks had assured him that the school district included this hotel and that there was no rush. She just wanted us kids to have room to grow. I was just enjoying the sunshine and the last few days of vacation.

    I was dreaming about tonight. I was going to stay up until dawn; Motel-boy and I had already started planning it. We'd found some firecrackers in one of the rooms we'd cleaned. Must've been left by that traveling salesman, they always leave something. Probably bought/ them in Tennessee and was gonna carry 'em north for the holiday. Kentucky had a law against fireworks except on the 4th of July, but down South, especially in Charleston, New Year's was a holiday everybody celebrated with fireworks and firearms, for that matter. One year I remember one of Eleanor's boyfriends bringing some M-80s by the apartment. He'd also brought sparklers for me and Agnes but was trying to impress Ellie by blowing stuff up. He probably would've made some time with her (They hadn't blown up the ivy plant that she'd nursed all summer long. Made a shambles of it, at least a thousand pieces! Motel-boy thought that was cool, but he couldn't get us any rifles or M-80s, which was probably a good thing. The firecrackers would probably do enough damage. I'd heard too many stories about drunk revellers firing off guns into the air and someone miles away ending up with a bullet in their scalp. I mean physics dictates that what goes up must come down, but down South, once a bullet leaves a gun, nobody really thinks about it again. Not having a gun, was okay by me.

Mr. Parks had the motel limo takes us to the convention center about seven. He instructed the driver to pick us up shortly after midnight so that the other paying guests would have the limo at their disposal later on when they'd need it. We were all pretty excited about riding in a limo for the first time, but you'd never know it by the way that Eleanor acted.

"I don't know why you're making me go to this thing, Dad," she moaned. "I can't imagine that I'm going to have any fun!"

"Eleanor," Dad cautioned, "don't make waves. Just sit back and enjoy the meal, find someone your own age, and hang out for a few hours. We'll be back at the motel right after the New Year, and you can do whatever it is that you feel the need to do then."

I'd never really imagined dad being a dad until he laid down the law with Eleanor. She'd been miserable since we came to Kentucky and even more so having to clean motel rooms for the cost of the room. I decided right then and there to make her evening an exciting one. I just had to figure out how.

Motel-boy was trying to catch my attention without catching anyone else's, and I saw him pull a lone firecracker out of his jacket. Yep, that oughta do it. If Eleanor was looking for fun, Motel-boy and I were going to provide it. Teenage boys and fireworks don't necessarily mix, but throw

Shockey

in a couple hundred drinking adults, and you have a recipe for disaster—or fun, depending on whose angle you're looking from.

The convention center was decorated with all kinds of balloons and streamers. It reminded me of my seventh birthday party, when Rita-mom decided to be a mom for a whole week. She'd decorated the house with streamers and balloons and invited a bunch of neighborhood kids over to play pin-the-tail on the donkey and eat cake and ice cream. She didn't have much experience being a mom, but she sure could decorate for a party. The convention center looked just like the house did except we were the only kids this time; the four of us, motel-boy and what seemed like every adult in Paducah.

There was a huge buffet when we walked in. Turns out the city threw around dozens of tickets to the hotel and motel people to hand out to guests so that the party would be a big success. Mr. Parks saved enough for his family and ours and all in all it was a pretty cool thing for him to do. The buffet, like I said, was huge. Just about everything you could imagine was on the tables stretching across one side of the ballroom. Mrs. Parks said they would keep the food on the buffet until about nine o'clock and then they'd clear away most of it, open a cash bar and let the dancing begin. She thought the girls would get a kick out of the dancing and told me and motel-boy that we could go up to the roof if we wanted. There was a small band performing up there, too, but it was more 'modern music.' Modern music? I'm not sure what she was thinking, but it sounded like what a mother would say. I just figured it would be a way to escape the family for a while. IVIotel-boy looked at me and winked, patting his jacket pocket. He and I were on the same wavelength.

The dinner would've been darn near perfect if Agnes hadn't insisted on sitting right next to motel-boy. He was still not sure how to take her and I think she made him more than a little uncomfortable. Anyway, motel-boy and I were on our way back from the buffet after our third or fourth trip and Agnes turned in her chair to say something chatty like, "Wow, I've never seen anyone eat so much and not show it!" She was being flirty again and it threw motel-boy off guard. He stammered for something to say and I piped up with, "Well, you eat like that all the time Agnes, and you don't show it." She was turning red but I couldn't stop, not yet, at least. I had to add, "Not yet, at least. I give you and then all hell broke loose. I didn't even get to finish my sentence when Agnes flew at me, claws out, screaming at the top of her lungs, "You rat! You dirty, rotten rat!" I was quick, growing up with all girls you learn to be, and trying to avoid her weapons, I spun a little to my right losing the tight grip I had on my plate and sending a half pound of peeled shrimp on top of motel-boy's sliced roast beef. Apparently, catching the extra weight threw him off, or maybe he was trying to send the shrimp back to my plate, but it all ended up half on the floor and half on Agnes. She managed to land one claw on my cheek, and the other nine careened down motel-boy's arm. She must've had her claws sharpened because motel-boy let out a shriek that could be heard above the din of a couple hundred adults eating, talking and banging around silverware. The shriek startled my dad and the Parks' so that in rising quickly, Mr. Parks caught part of the tablecloth and sent half of the plates and glasses to the floor. Mrs. Parks began yelling, "What happened? What happened!" and Dad, acting paternal, chimed in with "Kids! Kids!" Like that was going to help!

Immediately, wait staff from the convention center was on us like locust in a cornfield and it was all arms and legs, claws and shrimp. The melee didn't stop there, either.

Eleanor began wailing, "I can't even go out and have a good time, somebody always has to ruin things!"

Abbey was squealing her Abbey squeal and Agnes began sobbing. The whole thing would've been pretty funny if it hadn't ended with me getting socked in the jaw by motel-boy.

"Whatcha do that for?" I yelled while motel-boy was shaking his fist like he was trying to shake off red ants.

"Oh, my fist, my fist!" was all I heard. All I felt was my jaw, my poor jaw.

Agnes ran to motel-boy's aide and started applying ice that she'd scooped form one of the glasses that hadn't fallen wrapped in a napkin that had been dropped on the floor when Mr. Parks dumped the contents of the table.

"You poor thing," I kept hearing her say. "Let me take a look at that hand," she cooed while walking motel-boy toward the entrance of the ballroom.

Meanwhile, I was standing in a pile of shrimp and roast beef slices, my jaw throbbing. Dad was yelling, Eleanor was wailing, and Abbey was squealing as if she'd just finished Mr. Toad's Wild Ride. That was our family, alright. Some wild ride.

Mrs. Parks came to the rescue by taking Abbey by the hand and getting her under control. Dad tried to put Eleanor at ease, although I'm not sure why, nothing really happened to her! Agnes was playing Florence Nightingale to motel-boy and Mr. Parks was instructing the wait staff on clean up. Me? I just stood there, wondering if anyone would notice if I walked across the ballroom and out the front door. And into traffic. I didn't really want to, but it seemed like the thing to do.

Suddenly motel-boy caught my eye and jerked his head backward like he was trying to get me to follow him. He snatched his hand from the grasp of nurse Agnes, patted his pocket again and off we went. Agnes tried to follow, but dad caught up with her mumbling about Eleanor and Abbey and going home early. The argument Agnes started would keep him busy for a while so I hustled after motel-boy and wondered what was up his sleeve. I wasn't sure I really wanted to know. The boy could throw a mean punch, but somehow I knew it wasn't really meant for me, I just happened to get in the way.

Out in the foyer motel-boy began to apologize, "Sorry, man, I wasn't quite sure what to do and when your sister started clawing at my arm, it was just reflex. Your fat jaw just got in the way!"

"Yea, well, your fat jaw better not be anywhere near my fist next time it gets balled up, because payback sucks!" I didn't really use that term very often. Eleanor said it made you sound red neck, as if being from South Carolina didn't make that a given. But the term seemed totally appropriate here, and I slammed motel-boy on the back of the shoulder a little harder than he had anticipated, saying, "No big deal. I'm a man; I can take it!"

We both chuckled and motel-boy pointed toward the elevator, "Let's head up to the roof.'

"Better," I countered, "Let's hit the stairs. Agnes might follow and she'll never take the stairs, they'd make her sweat." We both laughed again and pushed through the doorway leading to the stairs, the roof, and a little mischief.

Chapter Five

THE PARTY ON the roof was more our speed. Most of the guests were college-age or late high school. There were a few adults, but generally, the crowd was unsupervised. The band was pretty good, too. At least they were playing music that we could appreciate. Actually motel-boy preferred country music, but I'd turned him on to a few rock and roll tunes that he liked and he looked like he was getting into the band. We were both scoping out the girls, hoping that we looked a little older than fourteen. Motel-boy was tall for his age and was beginning to sprout a little chin hair and it didn't look all that bad. I wore my hair pretty long and slumped a lot. Eleanor always said that girls didn't like boys that slumped, but I didn't care. I figured if I slumped, no one could see my face and guess my age. It seemed to work so far for me.

There was a buffet table on the roof, too. The food was simpler, chips, dip, meatballs, wings, but that was okay. I was working up an appetite again after the fiasco downstairs. I moseyed on over to the food table and reached for a plate. I wasn't really paying any attention when someone grabbed my wrist and shouted "Hey, what are you doing? This is a private party!"

I started to step back when motel-boy came to the rescue and said "No big deal, we were just leaving anyway. I was just looking for my girlfriend. I saw her come up here with some guy in a brown leather jacket. Seen 'em'?"

The girl turned to motel-boy and queried, "Brown leather? Was he wearing a Vertical Horizon t-shirt under it?"

Motel-boy mumbled, "I don't know but if I catch up with him, I'm gonna kick his ass."

"Oh, please, don't start any trouble. He's my boyfriend. Or, used to be, and you'll have to take a number!" She acted pretty ticked off, but she was still holding on to my wrist so I wasn't sure what to do. Suddenly she realized she was holding on to me and turned saying, "Oh, my apologies. This is my party. My dad owns the convention center and he wanted to be able to keep an eye on me. Of course, I haven't seen him all night long, just his goons — the guys in the red jackets. Pretty hard to miss, huh?"

She was talking to me and out of the corner of my eye, I could see motel-boy stepping back slowly, grinning. I guess he was giving me the go ahead, but I wasn't really sure.

"My name's Amanda, what's your's?" She was pretty, with shoulder length brown hair and green eyes, I think. I know she was still holding on to my wrist, though, so I felt compelled to answer her.

"I'm Shockey, and that's," and I turned to introduce motel-boy, but he'd vanished. Great; now what was I gonna do?

"Shockey? What an odd name? What's it short for," she asked, but I couldn't really answer. I kept concentrating on her hand wrapped around my wrist. I must have looked down at my wrist, because she immediately dropped it.

"Oh, I'm so sorry! You must think I'm a real dork!" She was staring at me. I couldn't help but notice that she was also a couple years older than me. I'm not sure how I knew, but growing up with sisters gives a fella a sixth sense about these things. I just knew she was older.

"My dad calls me Shockey because I have three sisters and he was shocked I was a boy. It's that simple and that stupid. Everybody calls me Shockey." It sounded stupid, but at least I'd answered her question without drooling all over her shoes. She was that cute.

"Do you mind if I get a plate of food? I was downstairs at the dance with some other people and my sister freaked out about something and I lost my plate of shrimp." It sounded plausible, especially since it was the truth, but it also gave me a reason for crashing her party.

"Oh, go ahead. I thought you were up here trying to start trouble." She was walking along the food table putting bits and pieces from every platter on a plate. "I just like having these parties and if things went as badly as last time, daddy said this would be the last."

Not only was she cute, but apparently she was loaded, too. This seemed like the perfect time to cut out and find motel-boy but I figured I'd better eat at least some of the food she was piling on the plate.

"Thanks, that's plenty." I reached out and took the plate from her. "Aren't you going to go try and find your boyfriend before my friend does?" I thought this would be a great excuse to get away from her before she discovered how young I was, but I was also worried about what motel-boy was up to. After all, he had a pocket full of illegal firecrackers. If he was going to have fun, I wanted to be in on it.

I took a few bites of meatballs and dripped some sauce on my chin. I tried to wipe it off with my sleeve but ended up knocking the plate of food off balance; presto, another pile of food on the floor. I had discovered my niche in life. I could spill a plate of food faster than you could say, "Holy crap, what's that noise!"

"Gun fire! Run! Everybody take cover!" Amanda was screaming and the boys in the band were tripping over themselves trying to run for the exit. Guests were running in pretty much the same direction, mainly because the wrong direction would sent them careening off the roof. The two exit doors were jammed with party goers and I could hear Amanda's voice above everyone else saying, "Quick! Inside!"

It suddenly occurred to me that we were not listening to the sound of gun fire, but motel-boy's early New Year's celebration. I started to chuckle and glanced around looking for my friend. It only took a few seconds to find him crouched down in a corner of the roof, close to a large potted tree. The crowd was thinning and slowing and naturally motel-boy had to toss a few more firecrackers off the rooftop to add just a little more confusion.

It really was quite funny, especially when he shouted out "Take that, you S-O-B, and leave my girlfriend alone!"

As quickly as the situation had begun, it was over, but a new turn of events was beginning as convention center security came busting through the crowd. Of course, they headed right my way because I was the only one not trying to leave the roof. Do you think I looked guilty enough?

The Red Jackets quickly secured me, arms in back, meatball sauce on my shoes and began screaming things like, "On your knees! Hands behind your back! Don't give us any trouble!"

Amanda turned to see me and ran over to plead my innocence, but it was a little too late and I was being escorted to the next best party in town and I could almost guarantee there wasn't going to be a buffet at this one.

As I was getting on the elevator with the Red Jackets I caught motel-boy out of the corner of my eye. All I could do was shake my head. He held his thumb and finger up to his ear like he wanted me to call him. Did he want me to call for bail? I was sure I was going to jail for the night. How did he plan on getting me out of this?

All the way down all I could hear was Jacket #1 asking my name and Jacket #2 asking where I lived. Did I know that firearms could not be discharged in the city? Did I have a permit? Where was my license? Where was the gun?

I started to laugh, but caught myself. I knew there was no gun so they couldn't prove that I had discharged one. But, then again, I had no license to prove who I was. I wasn't even old enough to have a permit! My dad was downstairs. Or, maybe he'd gone back to the motel. I was supposed to be with motel-boy. But, he was on the roof laughing his butt off at me getting arrested. It was his fault! He'd better help. Geez, how did I get myself into these situations? If I were in South Carolina nobody would've care if a gun had been fired. But I wasn't and apparently in Kentucky there wasn't the same level of celebratory fervor for New Year's. Heck, so far there wasn't a whole lot of anything I liked in Kentucky. Except maybe Amanda; but a lot of good that did me now. She thought my friend had shot her boyfriend!

Motel-boy must've taken the next elevator down because as I was standing at the side entrance to the convention center I saw him dash out the front door. Good. Maybe he was going back to the motel, spill his guts and rush down to the police station to rescue me. What was I thinking? He was going back to the motel all right, but it wasn't to save my butt. It was to save his!

At the police cruiser I was being frisked by Red Jacket #1 and #2 started asking questions again.

"What's your name, boy?" He was trying to sound all rough and tough, but at five foot eight and 235 pounds, I was guessing, he didn't exactly put the fear of God into me.

Jacket #2 was patting me down when he thrust his hand in my pocket and found the contraband. When motel-boy and I had been taking our cigarette break the day before, I had taken a second cigarette to try by myself at a later time. I'd also taken the lighter because motel-boy said he had so many of them. Harmless, I thought. In South Carolina everyone smokes. It stood to reason that Kentucky, being the tobacco-growing state that it was, would be just as tolerant. But, that's what I get for thinking. It seems that the smoking age in Kentucky is 18 and having a lighter is considered paraphernalia. The firearms charges would be easy to shake, but I'd been caught red-handed with a cigarette. Not that big a deal, to me. But with dad playing Mike Brady to Mr. and Mrs. Parks' Lois and Peter Griffin, it was going to be a tough sell to convince him it wasn't really mine. I couldn't very well say it was motel-boy's either. I wasn't really sure if the Parks' knew their son smoked, but it wasn't worth losing the only friend I had to rat him out.

I was stuck, faster than a flip flop in pluff mud. Man, oh, man, I was in trouble.

Chapter Six

THE TRIP TO the police station was quick. Actually, it seemed like it took forever, but it was only a couple blocks away. It was a substation, so there weren't a lot of other people around. I got taken inside to a waiting room that smelled like my old principal's office. I wasn't in there much, but I remember the smell and this place smelled the same, kind of like old clean.

The booking officer made me empty the contents of my pockets, that consisted of a pocket knife my grandfather had given me last time I saw him, turns out it was the last time anyone would see him, about seventy-five cents in change and chapstick. It was kind of embarrassing to be pulling chapstick out of your pocket when you're being booked on a firearms charge, but it was kinda cool, too. You know, like I was the bad boy that took care of his lips for the ladies. I was a real ladies man, too, that's for sure. That's why I was in the mess I was in. One minute I'm standing at a party with some pretty cool people, the cute girl who was throwing the party is chattin' me up and all I can do is worry about food, then I go and spill it. Wow, if that's not smooth . . .

I had my mug shot taken. I actually smiled for one of them and the officer taking the pictures made me take another one. A female officer did the finger printing. She kinda reminded me of Rita-mom. Her hair was the same color and her smile was similar. And I figured if she could smile, I guess it wasn't so bad that I had.

I got put into a holding cell which was really an 8' X 10' room with an iron door that had a sliding window in it. There were a few windows up high but there was no way to look out. I'm not sure I wanted to see out.

I kept imagining that I was being held by the Federales and that on the other side of the wall Pancho Villa waited with a get away horse. I guess I thought he was tying a rope around the window bars and was going to yank out the wall like they did in the old westerns, except that I was in Kentucky, not New Mexico and the jailhouse wasn't made of adobe, it was solid concrete. I'm pretty sure that Pancho Villa would've been noticed if he was hanging around a police substation in Paducah, Kentucky.

I waited for what seemed like hours before my dad and Mr. Parks came to pick me up. I thought my dad would be pretty mad, but I actually got more of a lecture from Mr. Parks. My dad really was new age from his marriage to his parenting skills. Mr. Parks, on the other hand was old school. Despite his son's looks, motel-boy really made his old man proud. I mean, the only thing I'd seen him do wrong in the week we'd been around was sneak a cigarette and set off firecrackers. What teen-age boy wouldn't do that? He worked hard at the motel and was generally respectful of all the guests. Anyway, Mr. Parks let me have it. He told me about how a friend of his had shot and killed his kid brother accidentally while playing with his old man's rifle and I got the feeling that this friend of his was pretty close, like maybe it was Mr. Parks or a cousin or something.

The lecture lasted longer than my incarceration and all the way back to the motel Mr. Parks kept yelling at me one minute and telling my dad it was going to be alright the next. He said he knew a lawyer that could help straighten it out and that we needed to get back to the motel. Apparently, everyone else had already gone back. Some New Year's Eve, huh? I never even got to tell dad and Mr. Parks that I didn't even have a gun and I guess I could've but I didn't tell Mr. Parks that it was his son who had the fireworks that the stupid Paducah police couldn't distinguish from actual gun fire!

I sure hated missing the New Year celebration at the convention center, but at least I had good fodder for my first day of school essay. You know the one, when you're a new kid in class and the teacher always asks you to "write a story about what you've been doing with your life so far." I hated those essays, although I had become pretty good at them.

Motel-boy razzed me quite a bit the next day. He hadn't meant to get me in trouble, but he didn't think I'd be a doofus and get myself arrested, either! We laughed about it, mainly because I didn't think anything bad was going to happen but also because we decided if I was going to start a new school in a couple of days, the best way to go in was as resident bad boy. It was a stretch, but I thought I could pull it off. Especially if I left my chap stick at home.

The rest of the day, we lounged around the motel-boy's room. The work department was slow because most of the guests were hung over from the night before or had already headed home. We slung a few bags of ice and then set back to eat some pizza and watch some movies.

The jury was still out on Kentucky, but some positive points were beginning to pile up.

Chapter Seven

THE FIRST DAY of school came and went without too many problems. I was assigned to motel-boy's homeroom, which turned out to be a mixed blessing. At least I knew someone, but he had some pretty weird friends and I was set to change my image. I didn't need any preconceptions based on the kid that I sat next to in homeroom.

My Chemistry class was interesting enough. Apparently one of the girls in my class had also witnessed the whole arrest thing a few days earlier at the New Year's rooftop bash. Her name was Carla and she happened to know XXXX from the party.

"So, you're 'Shockey,' huh?" She strolled up to me after the bell rang. "I heard you made some waves at the New Year's party."

She seemed nice enough, and cute, too, but I didn't really have time to rehash my New Year's fiasco, I was still trying to find my way around the gargantuan school I was to call home until dad decided to move again.

"I talked to XXXX and she got into some trouble because of you and the gun." Carla was, to say the least, blunt.

"Hey," it was time to defend myself, "I did not have a gun!" Word of caution: Never say the word 'gun' loud enough to be heard when walking down the hallway of a new school on the first day.

"So, you did have a gun! Is that why you were arrested? You had a gun?" Carla was not making this easy. She talked louder than I did and she was not listening!

"No!" I was really trying here, "I did not have a gun and I'll probably get out of all the charges." Geez, I had three minutes to get to my next class and I was having a loud, incriminating discussion in the hallway of a brand new school with a girl who would probably share the conversation with half of the eleventh grade before lunch."

"Hey," I'd love to share more of my life, but I have to find English Lit." I figured this was safe. Most freshmen didn't take English Literature and if she thought I was smart, maybe she'd leave me alone.

"With Mr. Osgood? No way! That's my next class, too!" Carla was overjoyed. Almost as much as I was. Geez, in less than a two-week period, I had moved, made a best friend, puked my guts out over a cigarette, gone uptown and 'downtown' and had met my personal tour guide of XXXX High School. Wow. My life was just getting better at every turn.

English Literature class was full of seniors who had put off taking the class until the last minute before graduation. This meant two things. Half of the seniors in the class were girls, of course that meant that the other half of the seniors were boys and by the looks of them mostly football players and wrestlers. It also meant that everybody had had a lot more English classes than I did. I wasn't sure if I was up to the pressure, but the guidance counselor had said that my earlier classes prepared me for the challenge. She also said for all the bouncing around I had done from school to school that my test scores were pretty good.

Mr. Osgood turned out to be a pretty cool guy. He was only about 30 or so and dressed somewhat like the students, only a little classier. He wore his pants just off his hips, but he wasn't bustin' the sag or nothing, and he'd spent a great deal more on his clothing than did most of the students. He also had longer hair. It wasn't all 1960s hippie like, but it was almost to his shoulders. I found out that most of the girls taking the class weren't watching the senior boys, but Mr. Osgood. He had a reputation as a ladies man and when he entered the room every girl began to swoon. That's an old-fashioned word Rita-mom uses to mean that the girls are all fluttery and flirtatious. Mr. Osgood had seen it all. His first rule on the blackboard was: Don't wear short skirts to class; if you do bring a sweater to put over your legs. Being it was January it wasn't too much of a problem yet, but one of the seniors sitting next to me, Ben Nalley, mumbled something under his breath about it being a warm winter and not having to wait for the spring fashions to break out.

"Good afternoon, ladies and gentlemen," Mr. Osgood was no nonsense from the start. "I have but very few requirements for this class, and since most of you," I don't know why but he looked directly at me as if he'd been told my whole life story all ready, "need my class to graduate, I don't usually have too many problems."

My face began to turn red which is a sure way to draw attention to your freshman self in a class full of seniors. Ben Nalley was the first to notice.

"Hey new kid," oh, great, now I was not only the guy with the red face but 'new kid' and in my book that was a sure fire miserable start to a new school.

"Heard all about you at XXXXX's party." He actually seemed to be impressed by the tone in his voice. "Way to impress the ladies, dude!" Okay, nice start. I was now 'dude' not bad. Not bad.

"Uh, it was all a mistake," was I lame or something? Here I had the perfect in with seniors and I was claiming it was a mistake? "I didn't really have a gun." Okay, the word gun would redeem me.

"Gun? Whoa, dude! Are you psycho or something?" Ben was holding his hands up and making his fingers into the shape of a cross. It seemed a great deal out of character based on my first impression.

"We're not worthy!" A few of the guys on the row next to the window all stood up and in unison dropped to their knees and began bowing.

"Guys! Guys!" Mr. Osgood was trying to take control of his class. "Back into your seats. Mr. Wallace? I have your add slip here." He was getting back to business quickly and I was impressed that the senior worshippers were instantly back in their seats without argument. "Stop by my desk after class and I'll give you a syllabus and class supply list."

Class supply list? I felt like I was back in third grade, but at least I was going to fit in. Who knew it might even be a good class.

Ben leaned over and whispered just loud enough for me and a few others close by to hear, "Dude, did you really have a gun?" When I walked into class everyone had been hanging around Ben like he was the most popular guy in school and now he was asking me to confirm something that would skyrocket my own personal social status. Quickly thoughts flashed through my head, pictures of me waving to crowds shouting adulations of 'Shockey is the best,' and 'Shockey rules!', but there were also pictures crashing into those of me in an orange jumpsuit picking up trash along 1-24 while carloads of classmates drove by waving and tossing drink cups from the windows. I had to answer, but my whole future at XXXXX was in the balance, so I did what any red-blooded American boy would do, I picked a fight.

"You talking to me? You better be able to back that up, low life!" I didn't really know what I was doing, but it was sure getting attention, especially from Mr. Osgood. Now to tell the truth, I'd only ever been in one other fight in my life and that was with Jo-Jo Sullivan down in Flagler Beach, Florida when I was in fourth grade. Jo-Jo was calling Agnes fat and I was taking up for my big sister. She wasn't fat and I wasn't going to stand for it. I do remember getting my behind pretty severely battered in that event, so my logic in calling out a huge senior in a brand new town on my first day of school was lost on me. Did it stop me? No!

"Who're you calling a low life, freak?" Ben was standing up and flexing some huge muscles and I was trying to think quickly. Mr. Osgood was making his way back through the desks yelling "Guys! Guys! Cut it out!" I was totally freaking out having started this chaos with absolutely no plan for ending it and my guardian angel stepped in and pulled the fire alarm.

B-r-r-r-rring-g-g-g-g! Oh, yeah! I was saved! Mr. Osgood flew back up to his desk, grabbing his roster and directing us out the door. "Single file! To the left, to the left!" Then he caught my eye and said "Wallace, by my side, pronto!" I was good. New town, new school, picked a fight over a non-deserved, but cool reputation, teacher's shadow during a fire drill. Yep. I'd pretty much trashed my future at this school for good. Maybe, Dad would decide to move again tonight. It wouldn't be too soon for me!

Chapter Eight

I SPENT THE afternoon in Mr. Wood's office. He was the principal and a pretty nice guy. He seemed like a fair person, so I was glad I was in his jurisdiction. I was afraid for a while that Mr. Osgood would take me up on my offer to fight Ben in retaliation for disrupting his class. Although, the way I figured it, he owed me. If I hadn't picked the fight with Ben, we'd have been in the middle of something really important and the fire drill would've disrupted it anyway. So, he owed me. I saved him from having to start over again. Okay, he didn't owe me that much. I was grabbing at straws. I was in deep ca-ca and I knew it. I was just going to have to take my lumps.

"Well, young man, some introduction to XXXX, huh?" Mr. Wood had a good demeanor. He was pleasant for an older gentleman. He wasn't really that much older than my dad, unless he used some of that hair formula for men to hide his gray hair. He was in pretty good shape, too. I don't think he would have been able to take Ben Nalley, but he could have held his own in pretty much any rumble. He was tall, too; about six-foot-five, by my estimates. Made a fella feel kinda small, but I guess that was pretty good for a principal. I had gone to one elementary school where the principal, Arnold Dibble was his name, was only about five-foot-five. There were a few six graders at that school who were almost as tall. We made fun of him all the time, but I didn't think Mr. Wood would have that same problem.

I guess he was expecting an answer, but I didn't know how to tell him that I hated moving, I was only hanging out with the only other male person I knew in Kentucky that wasn't related to me or renting me sleeping quarters. I also couldn't' tell him that motel-boy was responsible for the 'gun fire' at the convention center. Man, I was digging myself a hole I'd never get out of. I decided I had to answer, I just didn't know what I was gonna say until it came spilling out of my mouth.

"You know, you think you're a big man, being principal and all," what was I saying? Who was invading my body and making me say and do things that I never would have in South Carolina?

"Okay, okay, I see where you're coming from," Mr. Wood was pretty cool about my mouthing off and all. I began sliding deeper into my chair, trying to turn myself inside out so that, eventually, I would become invisible.

"I'm sorry," I mumbled. "I don't really mean to do stupid things. I think I was just trying to make a name for myself." Finally, the old Shockey was emerging from the multiple personality episode. "But, you know, you are kinda tall and that does make you a big man!" My attempt at humor had fallen flat. I wanted to die. And then Mr. Wood did an incredible thing.

"You wanna play some ball?" Mr. Wood began getting up from his chair behind his great big principal's desk and came around the side kind of leaning on the hand that was resting on the desk. He had his other hand propped on his hip and he was smiling at me. Smiling! I mean, give me a break. I'd almost started a fight and insulted the man and he was smiling at me?

"Uh, I guess so. What kind of ball?" I mean, basketball was okay and all maybe even catch with a baseball, but I had visions of Mr. Wood suiting up and taking me out for a game of football, one on one. That would be legal murder!

"Okay, grab your stuff, let's go to the gym." He took off his suit coat and folded it neatly and laid it on the back of his chair. He took off his tie and draped it over the suit coat. Then he started rolling up his sleeves and flashed two of the meanest looking tattoos I'd ever seen. One was a skull and crossbones with the Stars and Stripes furled and stuck through the center of the skull like it was going through ears. The other was three separate strands of barbed wire clenched in the middle with a bloody fist. Whoa!

"What's the matter?" Mr. Wood realized that I was staring at his tattoos.

"Uh, oh, nothing. Sorry." I didn't know what to say but I couldn't help but stare some more.

"You like that?" He pointed to the barbed wire tattoo. I just nodded in agreement and picked up my book bag to sling over my shoulder.

"Got that in Afghanistan. A buddy of mine was trying to scale a wall and messed up his hand pretty bad on some barbed wire. Got him sent stateside so we all had this tattoo done to remind us of him. It's kind of corny I guess, but Semper Fi and all." Mr. Woods had a soft side, even for a Marine.

"Why are you going to play ball with me?" I was in trouble, but I was being treated to a game of basketball.

"Well, I decided when I first started in administration that I was going to find another way to reach kids rather than the paddle." Mr. Woods went to a closet across the room and reached inside to grab something. He turned quickly and threw the basketball hard in my direction. I dropped my book bag and snagged the ball before it hit me.

"Good reactions. That says a lot about a kid. First off I know you're not into any kind of smoke. If you were high you wouldn't have been able to snag that ball. Now follow me." He opened the door to his office and looked at me. I grabbed my book bag, slung it over my shoulder and walked out. Mr. Wood shut the door behind me and followed.

"What's second?" I turned to face him and nearly ran smack into his huge chest.

"Second?" Mr. Wood looked down at me as if I was speaking a foreign language.

"You said 'first off' and then didn't continue." I was trying to figure out what was ahead of me. I sure didn't think we were just going to play ball.

"You'll find out." Mr. Wood just smiled and walked on ahead of me. His lanky legs covered twice as much distance as mine did in the same number of steps so it was a little hard to talk and walk at the same time. I was also having trouble keeping the book bag balanced on my shoulder, pack the basketball and talk so I just stopped talking. Maybe that's what he wanted.

We turned a couple of corners before we reached the gym. When we walked inside the girls were playing volleyball and there was Carla. She turned to stare at me and got beaned by the other team.

"Watch what you're doing!" the physical education teacher, Ms. Taylor, came running over as Carla dropped to the floor. "Everybody stop playing!"

Mr. Wood went sprinting across the gym and left me standing like a dork by the doors. I dropped my book bag and walked over, ball on hip, to see if Carla was all right. She was the only other student that I really knew at this school, so I guess she was kind of a friend. One of the other girls ran to the other edge of the gym.

"Get some water and a towel out of my office!" Ms. Taylor sounded serious, but then I heard her chuckle a bit so I guessed that Carla was okay. "She's gonna have a goose egg bigger than last time!"

Carla was sitting up by the time I got to her. Mr. Wood was kneeling behind her giving her some support. The girl that ran after the water and towel came up at the same time did and thrust the items at IVIs. Taylor.

"Here, Carla. Drink this!" Ms. Taylor took the water and twisted the cap off the bottle. She poured a bit of water into the towel first, then made a compress for the side of Carla's head. Mr. Wood sat back on the floor and began to laugh. Carla began to laugh while holding the towel to the knot on the side of her head. And I'm not sure if I joined in out of nervousness or friendship, but I began to laugh.

"Don't think I've forgotten about you, Wallace." Mr. Wood turned my direction and pasted a seriousness on his face that he missed in his office. I straightened right up and stopped laughing. I wanted to dribble the ball, but was afraid that he'd make me play him one-on-one in front of the girls if I did so I just held on to it. Pretty soon a group of boys came pouring into the gym and Ms. Taylor announced that class was over and sent the girls, all except Carla, back to the locker rooms.

There I stood. Mr. Wood was getting up and dusting off his pants. He began helping Carla up then turned to me. "Wallace? Help Carla into the locker room, then report back here pronto!" He sounded stern and I began to review the nervousness that I had earlier.

"Oh, and Wallace." Mr. Wood called after me.

I turned around and looked at him.

"No peeking." Then he grinned and crossed his arms across his chest.

I started back across the gym supporting Carla with my left arm and carrying the basketball with my right.

"And Wallace?" Mr. Wood called again. "The ball?"

I grinned, half turned and sent a three-pointer his way and sunk it right into his upturned hands.

"Good shot." He grinned back and I knew that things would be okay.

Chapter Nine

WEEKEND I COULDN'T come quick enough for me. The week had started out on a Wednesday and after only three days at school I was already known as a gunslinger, a smart aleck and a ladies man. I really only wanted to be known as Shockey Wallace, boy from South Carolina. I suppose if people knew more about me and my family, some of the names they stuck on me wouldn't stick so fast. I wasn't really ready to share the fact that Rita-mom thought she was going to be discovered by some Hollywood agent. My dad was making a name for himself, though. His first rough sketches of the sculpture were liked by the Paducah City Council. The mayor had even invited dad to a couple of events to show him off. I'm glad that dad hadn't tried to drag us along too. He usually tried to bring us kids because I think we gave him courage. He was more like one of us than our leader.

Eleanor was getting along well. She was a junior and had gotten to know Ben Nalley. I think she was caught in a discussion about me and identified herself as my sister at an inopportune time, but she ended up being a little sweet on Ben and I think that saved my neck. Agnes was a book worm and always hit it off with the librarians wherever we moved. She began volunteering after school with the media club so I got stuck picking up Abby and babysitting her a lot. I still managed to work around the motel, though. Mr. Parks had started slipping me a few bucks here and there. He said I was a good worker and kept motel-boy motivated. I slipped once and called his son 'motel-boy' to his face. I thought he'd be mad, but he just chuckled his Mr. Park' chuckle and went off to tell his wife. Motel-boy showed up at my room about 30 minutes later and wanted to know why I called him that. Truth is, I knew his name was

Kenny, but I'd just gotten in the habit of calling him motel-boy and the name was stuck in my brain now.

Abby liked her school. It was one of those arts-infused things where all the kids had lots of art and music classes and everything they did linked to something else they'd done in another class. The math and music classes swapped places all the time and the drama teacher, Mr. Rutledge, a little of the pretty-boy side for me, but a good teacher according to Abby and Agnes, who also volunteered at Abby's school once a week, had all the kids interested in writing and speaking. He would come up with plays about the pilgrims or the stock market crash or have the classes write short plays or poems about historical stuff. Agnes said she wanted to transfer there because the school had one class of every grade after sixth. I don't know if she ever talked to dad about it, but she would probably do pretty good at a school like that.

Anyway, it was Friday afternoon, the final bell had just rung and I didn't have a thing to do until Sunday afternoon, when it was my turn to clean the parking lot and front walkway. Agnes had gotten a ride to Abby's school and was taking her home and watching her. They were working on some dramatic presentation together. Sounded boring to me. Eleanor had a date with Ben Nalley and that left the motel room empty until someone came home. If I only got twenty minutes of peace and quiet it would be worth a million bucks.

I decided to skip the bus ride home and walk. It was only about 15 blocks and traffic was light crossing Hinkleville Road that time of afternoon. I was walking along and thinking about everything that had happened and someone called my name.

"Hey, Shockey!"

I didn't quite recognize the voice, but it was female. I was almost afraid to turn around but another voice followed.

"Hey, motel-boy!" I knew that voice, it was the real motel-boy. What was he doing calling me that?

I turned around quickly and started to speak when I saw motel-boy and Carla half running to catch up.

"Wait!" motel-boy was persistent, and since he was going my way, and really my only friend, I stopped.

"Why aren't you riding the bus?" Good question.

"Oh, I just decided to walk home and think about my week so far." Lame excuse, but it was the truth. "Why are you walking?"

"Well, this sweet young thing stopped me in the hallway and wanted to know if I knew anyone who wanted to go to the movies tonight and I got to thinking about my southern buddy with no social skills." Motel-boy sure had a way with words. Unfortunately, most of the time, his way was way off base.

"Hey, how's the head?" Carla just grinned at me so I turned my attention to motel-boy. "Speaking of no social skills, whatcha wanna see?" I answered with a little hesitance. There were a couple of good movies at the mall down the road from us and since Mr. Parks had been paying me I had a little bit of change saved up. I wanted to buy a bike, but I was willing to part with some savings to buy a change of scenery.

"We're thinking about Scare Me 11, it is supposed to be way better than Scare Me." Motel-boy was fun to be around and I loved a good horror flick so I agreed.

"Sure," what time does the show start? I managed to catch Carla watching me out of the corner of her eye. She was standing close to motel-boy but they weren't touching or anything. And, before I knew it another body entered the picture.

"I think the first show is at seven," it was Chelsea Barber. She was a tenth grader but I'd heard motel-boy talk about how they'd kinda gone steady in sixth grade and by the looks of things she was interested in round two.

"Hey, baby!" Smooth, motel-boy, smooth. "I waited for you outside the gym but coach told me to leave school grounds so I figured you'd catch up." She walked up to him and planted a little peck of a kiss on his cheek. Okay, if they were a couple, I guess that meant Carla was supposed to tag along with me. Or, me with her, whatever. Either way we were a foursome, at least for this afternoon and evening. I kinda liked the company on the way home anyway. It was a bus ride with all the gossip, but none of the bus.

We decided to see another movie 'Oops," about a kid that was always getting into some kind of mess or making a mess of somebody else's business. It sounded like my life story this past week so I wanted to see it just to commiserate with the main character. Chelsea said she'd heard it starred some teen-age heartthrob and she never missed his movies, emphasis on his. Carla said she didn't care, but I caught her looking at me again, so I think we could've watched one of those health class films and she'd have said okay just to be with me. I don't wanna sound all egotistcal or nothing, but she was staring at me a lot! And she was kinda cute.

We ended up walking to the movies. Carla's mom brought her a change of clothes by the motel and picked up her book bag and Chelsea's gym bag — she never seemed to have books, only cheerleading stuff— and told the girls she'd pick them up at the mall at 11. My dad was going to be out until late and Agnes was cool with watching Abbey so I was ready to enjoy a full evening of company without any disruptions. The walk wasn't bad and the girls were pretty good company. They did all the talking, but half way to the theater I got to thinking about Mr. Wood. We never did get to play that game of one-on-one. I was wondering how good a shot he was. I guess I started thinking out loud because Carla started answering my thoughts.

"Oh, Mr. Wood used to play for our high school. He was All County, All Region, All State and even played on some team made up of players from Kentucky, Tennessee and Illnois his senior year. It was some big deal 'cuz he used to have framed clippings of it on his wall." Carla was a wealth of knowledge about Mr. Wood. Turns out he was a neighbor of hers and knew her mother back in high school.

"Oh, Mr. Wood, is too dreamy!" Chelsea thought every male between the ages of thirteen and thirty-three was dreamy. Mr. Wood was a little out of that age range, but I'd heard several girls comment about how they thought he was good looking. I wasn't a good judge of looks. I had blonde hair, but it was kind of moppish looking. I hated haircuts pretty much kept a half tan all year, at least I used to living near the ocean. I didn't think I really looked the surfer part, but some kid at school the first day called me 'surfer dude.' Mr. Wood on the other hand was tall and muscular. I thought he'd been in the military, but he went to college to play ball and then when the pros didn't draft him came back to Paducah to teach. Guess we were pretty lucky.

"Mr. Wood is really funny, too," Chelsea was gushing again. "He came to school dressed in a dinosaur costume a couple years ago when he was at the middle school."

Frankly, I couldn't imagine that. A six-foot plus dinosaur walking the halls of any middle school was kinda scarey!

"The kids promised to read 10,000 books one year on the promise that if we did, Mr. Woods would come to school as a Tyaranus, a tyranny, oh, you know," Chelsea was not the brightest bulb on the string.

"T-Rex, silly," Carla was, however. "Tyrannosaurus Rex to be exact!" She was cute and smart.

"Yeah, whatever, anyway, we read more than 10,000 books and Mr. Wood walked around all day eating a big smoked turkey leg. He was so funny! A dog even nto the school}' Chelsea paused.

"Oh, it was Mrs. Wykes' Jack Russell! I remember!" ml)tel-boy was getting into the conversation now. "And he followed Mr. Wood around. Don't you remember, Mrs. Wykes had taken him to the vet and he was wearing that silly white collar thingy and everytime he barked it was like he was using a megaphone." Motel-boy began laughing hysterically, "and then he peed on Mr. Wood's leg!"

"Oh, yeah," Carla was joining in now. I felt a little left out, but the picture they painted was pretty comical. She added, "He just hiked his little leg and let it go, all over that rented costume! I've never seen Mr. Wood so mad!" The whole group was laughing now. The three of them because they'd been there; and me, because I was really enjoying myself.

The movie turned out to be pretty good, too. I stuffed myself with popcorn and Sugar Babies and Carla, turns out, is diabetic, so she didn't have anything but a three-dollar bottle of water. Good thing because I was running low on funds after just one outing. Carla actually offered to pay for her own water, but it just seemed natural to say "I'll get that."

Chapter Ten

A WEEK LATER, 1 was sitting in Mr. Osgood's class, glad I'd smoothed his ruffed feathers. Carla had started sitting by me. Not being a pest or anything, but making it obvious that she liked me. She never offered to be my partner in any group or pair stuff, but she always waited at the door for me after class and we'd walk to her next class, which happened to be next to my Chemistry class. We weren't really a couple or anything, we just hung out together a lot.

My dad was making progress on the sculpture. He was supposed to create a depiction of some Indian motioning toward the Ohio River. It was some historical gesture of when an Indian named Paduke offered assistance to the settlers who were coming to Western Kentucky. Agnes looked up the event and was telling us all about it at dinner one night, but I don't remember what she was saying. Wish I'd listened more carefully.

"Mr. Wallace? Are you with us?" Mr. Osgood was talking to me but I wasn't quite hearing what he said.

"Surf dude!" Ed Grimes, the boy that gave me the nickname, was shouting across the room, "Tell 'em about your old man! He's like carving this Paduke dude outta stone, man!" His voice was from California, but he was born and raised on 10th Street in downtown Paducah. He was sent to XXXX because he'd been in a lot of trouble at his old high school and the school district was trying to keep down the number of expulsions. The jury was still out whether or not Ed was a good candidate for the intervention program. I only knew so much about him because Ms Roberts, my Spanish teacher was his mentor. She liked to talk about the other students without giving up their names, but everyone always knew just who it was. She called Ed "that troubled boy from another culture." Ed was white, his parents were poor and he lived downtown, way other culture if you ask me.

Anyway, Mr. Osgood had been talking about early settlers and all the tough times they had with Indians and then he said something about Paduke and turned the whole class' attention to me.

"Shockey? Are you with us today?" It was more prodding than surprise, and I was really trying hard to think about what Agnes had said. Something about the Cherokee Indians in the area helping out with food and protection from the Apache over the river in Missouri or maybe it was about food during a long, cold winter. Maybe I was confusing my pilgrims with my Kentucky settlers, anyway, I realized the whole class was staring at me.

Carla had her hand cupped around her mouth saying something in a whisper. "Chief Paduke welcomed the settlers to his village and helped care for the sick."

I could barely make out what she was saying and I found myself leaning over slighty and squinting to see her lips moving better. Apparently I was leaning too hard and I fell out of the side of my desk, hooking my left leg under Lisa Wainwright's chair in front of me and nearly tipping over her desk, too. I wound up on the floor beneath my desk and books staring straight into the face of Carla and Mr. Osgood, who had come crashing to the back of the room over chairs and desks.

Carla finished her sentence, but a little louder, "Chief Paduke welcomed the settlers into his village," and then the whole class chimed in.

"And helped care for the sick!" It was embarrassing.

Lisa was scowling at me. Carla had a look of desperation, as in, 'How could I like someone who is such a doofus,' and almost every guy in the class was rolling on the floor or clutching a side laughing. Please add 'class clown' to my growing resumé. Just when I thought things couldn't get worse, Mr. Wood poked his head into the room and announced in his super-jock voice, "Shockey, come with me, please." For the life of me I couldn't imagine what was wrong. I mean, I had just caused the meleé in

English, so that couldn't have gotten back to Mr. Wood so quickly. There had to be something wrong with my family, something more wrong, than the obvious. I picked myself up with the help of Carla and a couple of others, looked around the room and headed down the hallway, following quickly after Mr. Wood. My mind was working at warp speed and I couldn't imagine what was going to happen.

I walked through Mr. Wood's door and immediately saw dad sitting in the chair across from that massive desk. He didn't look none too happy and if I didn't know better I would've sworn that he'd been crying. He always said that men needed to keep in touch with their sensitive side, but sometimes I thought his sensitive side kept him from being a real man, especially when it came to his kids.

"Come in, Shockey. Have a seat there next to your father." Mr. Woods seemed serious, too.

"So, what's up? Why are you here, Dad? One of the girls sick?" I tried to sound like it was no big deal, but in nine years of school, I don't remember dad ever showing up without a reason, like moving us the next day or registering us for that day. I mean, dad just didn't do the whole PTA school volunteer thing. I don't think he ever even made it to a teacher conference, not that any ofus ever had any problems that needed a conference.

"Sit down, Shockey," Dad was sounding really bad.

"I am sitting, what you want me on your lap?" Maybe a little humor would help the situation.

"I talked to your mother today. Dad was staring at the floor and even he usually looked us right in the eye. He said anyone that couldn't look you in the eye couldn't be trusted. It wasn't that I didn't trust my dad, but I was getting worried, now.

"She's leaving me . . . uh . . . us . . . she's got a job in the movies down in South Carolina and she says it's going to Hollywood when her shoot is over. She says she wants a permanent split." Dad's voice was shaking as he spoke.

Shockey

"You mean a divorce? Rita-mom wants a divorce?" Now my voice was shaking. I mean she wasn't around much anyway, but she was our mother and she did occasionally drop in.

"That's not the worst of it. She wants to take Abbey with her." That's when Dad really broke down. Right there in front of Mr. Wood. It was bizarre I didn't know what to do. I wanted to hug my dad, I wanted to wipe his tears. I also wanted to punch him in the shoulder and yell, 'Get over it, dad!' but mostly, I wanted to run out of the office, down the hallway and out of X and never look back. I didn't think life could get any worse for me, but it just had. What was our family going to be like without Abbey? And could Rita-mom just swoop down from whatever nest she was hiding in and take one of the children she repeatedly abandoned? I wasn't gonna let it happen!

"Mr. Wood, I need to leave. I'm not going back to class. My dad needs me." I stared out the window past Mr. Wood but heard him say he agreed.

"Sure, Shockey. I'll tell Mr. Osgood and the rest of your teachers. Go on home. Take care of your dad." He stretched his hand out to me and turned to Dad, but he was a basket case. I just needed to get out of there.

"Come on dad, let's go get Abbey." We walked toward the door and I never felt so confused.

Chapter Eleven

SITTING AROUND THE motel room was weird. Agnes was punching out every pillow in the place. Dad was still crying and Eleanor was cleaning every inch of the room then starting all over again. Abbey was being very quiet. She wasn't sure what to expect, but dad had already talked to Mr. Parks and he had a lawyer friend of his who was going to help us out.

None of us was really worried about the divorce. That wouldn't change anything. Dad took care of us, paid our bills and provided stability, what little of it we had. Rita-mom just drifted in and out of our lives whenever it was convenient for her. She missed every birthday I ever had, or at least the ones I remember. She'd made it to Eleanor's twelfth birthday, but had made a mess of it trying to be like a movie star whipping her sunglasses on and off. She couldn't even get Eleanor and Agnes' names right. Eleanor was so embarrassed that she spent half the party in her bedroom. She'd invited a couple of friends over and they ended up going home early. Birthdays weren't done very well in our house and I don't really remember having any other parties; except maybe for Abbey. She was everybody's favorite. We all knew that fall that Rita-mom showed up something strange was going on.

She stuck around for six or seven months, or so, delivered Abigail and left about two months later. Dad had said that she'd stuck around while Eleanor and Agnes were babies and when I came around she was intrigued by a boy baby so she helped out with me, too. But with Abbey we always had questions and no one wanted to answer them so we took her under our wing and made her the best little sister you could have. And she was good, and cute and smart. She made us all proud. Rita-mom never really seemed to care.

Shockey

If Rita-mom took her away it would destroy the whole family, especially dad. He knew Abbey was a blessing, she represented that last fall Rita-mom had been part of the family and dad wouldn't let her go without a fight. Mr. Parks was going to help out, too. A knock on the door shook me out of my pity party.

"Hey, motel-boy, mom wanted you guys to have some food, so she made sandwiches and brownies and wants to know if you still want sugar in your tea and all." It was the real motel-boy and he'd taken to calling me the same weird name. I don't know if it was to get me to call him Kenny or if he just thought he was funny. I took the basket and thanked him.

"Thanks, dude. You wanna come in or somethin'?" I knew he wouldn't, but I had to ask. I hadn't seen him since I was pulled out of Mr. Osgood's class and I'm pretty sure no one knew why I didn't come back. Kenny only knew because of his dad. I handed the basket off to Agnes and darted out the door after him.

"Kenny!" I hadn't used his name before and it felt weird. "Wait up!"

"You called me by my name . . . what gives?" Kenny wheeled around and looked at me like I'd just given him tickets to the Super Bowl.

"Well, you know you are like my only . . . my best friend up here and I just don't feel like sitting around the motel room with everybody crying and all." I just needed some companionship and boys are pretty good about just hanging out without having to bear their souls or anything creepy like that.

"My dad told me about your mom." Kenny was trying to have a conversation, but I wasn't really listening.

"Do you think that Mr. Wood told anyone else?" I was really more concerned with what everyone would think than I should have been. Who cared, anyway? I mean most of the kids I knew anywhere we lived had divorced parents. What was the big deal?

"My dad's lawyer, Mr. Moreau, is pretty good. He's been a lawyer for a long time and is pretty successful." Kenny was trying to be up beat, but I was still really bummed.

Kenny continued, "He's even got his own commercials on television. They have some little ditty like 'If your spouse is on the loose then call Moreau to cook their goose!'" Kenny's singing was pretty weird, but the funny song made me feel a little better anyway.

"How long have your parents been married?" I was just searching for anything to talk about.

"Oh, something like 30 years." Kenny was kicking rocks sideways into the flower beds. "I have an older sister." Kenny paused for a moment then continued, "And brother, but they haven't lived here for about 10 years." I was also learning something about Kenny now.

"I didn't know you had any siblings," I said.

"Yeah, Karen is 29 and lives somewhere in Arizona with her Air Force husband. They don't have any kids and I think they like it that way." He was pretty nonchalant about not having much contact with his sister.

"What about your brother?" I was venturing into the thin ice of deeper friendship.

"Oh, Ronnie? He's dead." Kenny was still kicking rocks, but the last one was kicked a little harder than the rest of them. I thought I'd hit a nerve.

"Sorry, didn't know." I didn't wanna fall through that ice I'd just ventured onto.

"Yeah, well, it happened when I was about three and we don't really talk about him much." Kenny stopped kicking rocks and just stared at the highway watching the cars passing by.

"He was sixteen and was on his way to play in a basketball game for XXXXX when he tried passing another car and was hit head-on by a truck coming the other way. He died at the accident and my mom and dad don't talk about it because they'd had a fight with Ronnie before he took off. They think he was driving fast because he was mad at them." Kenny shoved his hands in his pockets and looked down at the parking lot, playing with a rock with the toe of his shoe. "About a year after that Karen got married and moved away. She and Mike don't have any kids and we don't see them much because of where they live. I'm pretty much all my parents have left, but they're good to me. I guess that's why they want to help your dad keep Abbey so close." I decided that was why they were so good to us. They liked having children around again.

To tell you the truth, Kenny was pretty normal to have all that crap going on in his childhood. Made me like him a lot more, too. When I first met him I figured he was spoiled having the run of the motel and all, but he was turning out to be a pretty cool guy.

We were on our way to the office to see what was in the courtesy cabinet where Mrs. Parks kept all the cookies and brownies for the guests when we saw a familiar SUV hit the parking lot. The truck stopped and out jumped Carla. She came running over to me, slinging her arms around my neck squealing, "You're all right! You're all right!"

"Yeah, I'm all right, but are you?" It was kinda weird having her hanging on me. "What are you doing here, anyway?"

"When you didn't come back to class, I got worried and I was watching out the window when I saw you and your dad walking across the front lawn." She was truly acting concerned, but I still was new at this boyfriend thing so I didn't know how to act.

"Yeah, well there's this stuff going on with my family and," I wasn't sure what to say next. I didn't really want to share the whole story, but I was kinda glad she'd stopped by and all.

Kenny piped in, "It's his dad. He got some bad news about his health. That's what's up. He'll be okay so you can go on home now, Carla. I've got his back." Way to go Kenny!

"Kenny Parks, you are such a liar!" Carla was all girl, you couldn't get anything past her. "I know his father is fine but there is something wrong! Now, spill it motel-boy!" Carla looked me dead in the eye and called me 'motel-boy' and it threw me for a loop.

"What did you just call me?" I was totally off guard by her remark.

"Motel-boy, why?" Carla turned toward Kenny and stuck her finger right at his nose, "He told me to call you that!"

I glared at Kenny and felt like punching him out but then it hit me about how funny the 'motel-boy' thing had been and I began to smile. I looked at Kenny and he was grinning, too, and then I turned to look at Carla and she threw her arms around me and hugged me like she had when she first arrived.

"Oh, Shockey! Everything will be okay, I promise!" Carla sounded sincere, but I felt compelled to tell her just how send us everything was.

"Yeah, well Mr. Parks has a lawyer that my dad can talk to and we're going to do everything we can to make sure that Abbey doesn't leave." I opened my mouth and everything just started pouring out like rainwater in a flooded ditch.

"Abbey! Oh, no! She can't leave!" Carla began to tear up and it was clear that she was really wrapped up in my family. She'd met them several times and had gotten along pretty well with all three of the girls. She was even the one that helped Eleanor and Ben Nalley hook up for good. Seems most of the money in Paducah lived near Carla.

Something made me hug Carla back and I spoke in a low voice so only she could hear, "Nobody's taking Abbey, not as long as I'm around."

Chapter Twelve

IT WAS ABOUT a week after I'd heard the news about Rita-mom and her plans. Dad had talked to Mr. Moreau, and he was pretty confident that since she'd never spent more than a few weeks at most with the family, family court judges in Kentucky would view Dad's retaining parenting rights. It all meant that Abbey would probably stay with us. The court case was set for March 1, and Dad was having a hard time keeping his mind on his sculpture. Mr. Parks had arranged for dad to take a little time away from his project. He'd been ahead of schedule and the mayor was pleased with his work, so it didn't take much convincing, but now he was around the motel a bunch and that limited my privacy a lot.

Kenny and I had been hanging out a lot more, too. Mr. Parks kept us both busy with things to do around the office. He wanted us to start painting lawn furniture and getting the pool deck ready to paint. He said spring was right around the corner, and he needed to be ready for all those out-of-town relatives coming to high school graduations. It seemed kind of silly, but we had had a mild winter and getting stuff ready for spring and summer was a great way to keep my mind off our family troubles.

Dad had received some legal papers in the mail. One set talked about a paternity test and Eleanor had said that would determine whether or not Abbey actually belonged to our family. Of course, she belonged! She was our little sister! But Eleanor said it was more complicated than that and I just walked away because I didn't want to hear about 'more complicated,' my life was complicated enough. I liked Paducah and I was afraid that if dad lost Abbey in a court battle with Rita-mom he would be inclined to pull up stakes and head to some other town. The next one might not be as friendly as Paducah had been. I also wouldn't have a friend as good as

Kenny. He was the first real friend I'd ever had and I didn't want to give him up anymore than I wanted to lose Abbey.

Agnes got a job at the mall and had been buying us all new clothes with her discount. She wanted to make sure we all looked good when we showed up in court. Mrs. Parks said that we probably wouldn't all have to go, but then Mr. Parks had mentioned that the lawyer said it could be in dad's favor if we all took turns talking at the hearing. All I could think of was the old Perry Mason reruns we'd seen on cable; the bigger-than-life lawyer swaggering into a black and white court room while his pretty secretary scribble notes at a massive oak desk. Then there was the craggy old prosecutor who sat across the room hurling threats and mean comments at the defendant. I kept picturing dad on the witness stand covered with flecks of clay, his hair all tossled and the four of us scattered on the floor around the bailiff begging for forgiveness. It was really Dickinsian and a little over the top.

Kenny told me he'd been cruising the internet and found out that a lot of states honour custodial-parent relationships as much as blood ties. It was all too weird for me and I found myself wanting to move to escape. I suddenly understood a little about why dad kept moving us around so much. I think he was just trying to escape the inevitable — Rita-mom coming around and wreaking her emotional havoc.

Eleanor spent a lot of time reading extra stories to Abbey, and Agnes continued to shower her with gifts. Dad actually went back to work after about three days. He said he needed to stay busy and not one of us disagreed. I went back to school and Carla kept following me around, but if I was her boyfriend, I didn't really feel like it these days. I felt like a little kid that had just found out that Santa didn't really exist. I had a lump in my throat and knots in my stomach. I tried to figure out how I could help dad and nothing was coming to mind. I'd never felt so useless in all my fourteen years.

Abbey knew something was going on, but I think she was the most stable of all. She continued to bring home artwork for the refrigerator in the Parks' apartment. The mirrors in our room, as well as the small fridge we had, were already covered with pictures of the family, a dog we all wanted but knew we'd never have and beach scenes. Some of those pictures made me sad for South Carolina, but Abbey said she drew them to help me remember what it looked like. Kind of like Rita-mom; just when we all began forgetting what she looked like, she'd rear her head and appear for a day or two. I wish she'd never found us this time around.

Author Biography

Laura Turok-Ellis was educated in Kentucky and graduated from Western Kentucky University in 1979, only to enter the world of journalism through radio, television, and finally newspapers. She has written innumerable news stories, feature articles and more than her share of special sections blurbs about anything from hunting dogs to manufactured housing. She most enjoys writing for pleasure and has produced her first book efforts as a result of many hours of hounding by her friends and colleagues. Laura tends to write using bits and pieces of people she knows and is comfortable grafting her characters into familiar places in her memory. Laura's interests, besides writing, include, gardening, any water sports, rambling through the myriad 'antique' shops that abound in South Carolina and cooking. She hopes one day to publish a cookbook of family recipes. Laura lives in Charleston, South Carolina with her two sons, Riley and Charles and two dogs, Cooper and Hershey, and often visits her daughter Christina and her family, which includes James and their dog Duke.